7523 9102

SPECIAL REPORTS

THE CHARLOTTESVILLE
PROTESTS

BY MICHAEL CAPEK WITH DUCHESS HARRIS, JD, PHD

Essential Library

An Imprint of Abdo Publishing | abdobooks.com

abdobooks.com

Published by Abdo Publishing, a division of ABDO, PO Box 398166, Minneapolis,
Minnesota 55439. Copyright © 2019 by Abdo Consulting Group, Inc. International
copyrights reserved in all countries. No part of this book may be reproduced in
any form without written permission from the publisher. Essential Library™ is a
trademark and logo of Abdo Publishing.

Printed in the United States of America, North Mankato, Minnesota
082018
012019

Cover Photo: Chet Strange/Stringer/Getty Images News/Getty Images
Interior Photos: Shay Horse/NurPhoto/Sipa/AP Images, 4–5, 10; Joel Carillet/
iStockphoto, 12–13; UW Madison/iStockphoto, 17; Mel Evans/AP Images, 19; Red Line
Editorial, 25; Ryan M. Kelly/The Daily Progress/AP Images, 28; Steve Helber/AP
Images, 33; Adam Anderson/Stringer/Reuters/Newscom, 34–35; AP Images, 36–37;
iStockphoto, 42, 92–93; Scott Threlkeld/AP Images, 44–45; Albin-Lohr-Jones/Sipa/
AP Images, 46–47, 73, 88; Chip Somodevilla/Getty Images News/Getty Images, 51;
Jason Andrew/Getty Images News/Getty Images, 54; Cliff Owen/AP Images, 57;
Michael Nigro/Pacific Press/Sipa USA/AP Images, 58–59, 65, 68–69, 80–81, 87;
Virginia State Police/UPI/Newscom, 67; Sue Ogrocki/AP Images, 76; Ty Greenless/
Dayton Daily News/AP Images, 78; Ted S. Warren/AP Images, 90–91; Calla Kessler/
The Washington Post/Getty Images, 98

Editor: Alyssa Krekelberg
Series Designer: Maggie Villaume

Library of Congress Control Number: 2018948237

Publisher's Cataloging-in-Publication Data

Names: Capek, Michael, author. | Harris, Duchess, author.
Title: The Charlottesville protests / by Michael Capek and Duchess Harris.
Description: Minneapolis, Minnesota : Abdo Publishing, 2019 | Series: Special
        reports set 4 | Includes online resources and index.
Identifiers: ISBN 9781532116766 (lib. bdg.) | ISBN 9781532159602 (ebook)
Subjects: LCSH: Race relations--Juvenile literature. | Protest movements--United
        States--Juvenile literature. | Soldiers' monuments--Southern States--Juvenile
        literature.
Classification: DDC 976.106--dc23

CONTENTS

CHAPTER ONE

UNITE
THE RIGHT

F riday evening on August 11, 2017, a group of approximately 250 men and women gathered in Charlottesville, Virginia. They met in a dark field on the campus of the University of Virginia (UVA). At around 8:45 p.m., they set out in a long line, carrying flaming kerosene torches. Organizers shouted instructions. "Stay in formation! Two by two! Now! Now! Go!"[1]

The well-ordered group snaked across the historic university campus, much of it designed by the school's founder, Thomas Jefferson. As they marched, many people in the crowd chanted, "Blood and soil" and "You will not replace us."[2]

Alt-right protesters circled counterprotesters at the Thomas Jefferson statue.

Those words are rallying cries often used by members of various organizations that support white supremacist causes. These groups and individuals are sometimes referred to as the alt-right. Members of these groups share specific racist, white supremacist, and populist beliefs. They frequently choose threatening and sometimes violent tactics to express their point of view. Such behavior has led the Federal Bureau of Investigation (FBI) and numerous civil and human rights organizations to label them as hate groups.

The demonstrators were in Charlottesville for a rally they called Unite the Right. It was scheduled for the next day at noon in nearby Emancipation Park, formerly called Lee Park. Their stated purpose was to protest a recent vote by the Charlottesville City

WHAT DOES "BLOOD AND SOIL" MEAN?

The slogan "blood and soil" represented a principal idea of the Nazi Party during the 1930s. This group, led by dictator Adolf Hitler, controlled Germany before and during World War II (1939–1945). Hitler depicted native-born Germans as national heroes. These Germans stood in sharp contrast to foreign-born Jewish bankers and merchants. Hitler said that Jewish bloodlines were impure. He claimed their greed and dishonesty was responsible for all of Germany's and the world's problems. He used it as an excuse to murder millions of Jews and non-Germans in Europe. People who shouted "Blood and soil!" in Charlottesville were essentially stating their belief that Hitler was correct in connecting a racial identity ("blood") with a location of birth ("soil").[3]

Council. Several weeks earlier, the council announced its decision to remove the statue of Robert E. Lee, a Confederate general from the Civil War (1861–1865), and to rename the space Emancipation Park.

The city council reluctantly granted permission for the rally on Saturday, August 12. However, the Friday night demonstration was not part of the agreement. Police came to monitor the situation but did nothing to stop it. Officials decided to allow the demonstrators to exercise their constitutional rights of free speech and peaceful assembly.

That didn't make things any less tense or potentially explosive. As the rowdy, torch-bearing protesters neared the statue of Jefferson in the center of the UVA campus, they were confronted by a much smaller group of counterprotesters. Many of them were students and local residents. They joined hands, encircled the statue, and displayed a large sign saying, "UVA Students Act Against

WHO STARTED THE UNITE THE RIGHT RALLY?

The rally in Charlottesville was initially organized by Jason Kessler, a Charlottesville resident known for his racist website and opinions. He strongly objected to the vote by city leaders to remove the statue of Robert E. Lee. He and other white supremacists communicated and set up the Charlottesville protest activities online. Those who opposed this rally monitored Kessler's websites and organized a counterprotest.

STATUES OF DISCORD?

The action by Charlottesville city leaders to remove the Robert E. Lee statue and rename the park was part of a nationwide movement. Many cities have begun to remove statues and symbols glorifying the Confederacy and its leaders. Because the Civil War was fought over slavery, many people regard Confederate monuments as blatantly racist symbols and want them removed. White supremacist organizations have protested, sometimes violently, in favor of keeping them.

White Supremacy."[4] They faced the noisy protesters as the protesters approached and surrounded them.

Shouting, threats, and name-calling intensified as the two groups pressed closer and closer together. Angry people bumped and jostled one another. Someone threw a punch. Immediately, the area erupted into a wild brawl. People swung and threw lighted torches at each other. Pepper spray sent protesters from both sides scurrying to find medical assistance. Police moved in and began separating combatants, several of whom were led away in handcuffs. Scuffles and shouting continued as people from both sides of the confrontation moved apart.

In a Facebook post, Charlottesville's mayor, Mike Signer, blamed the ugly incident on the intimidating behavior of white supremacists. The protest had, after all, appeared without permission on the UVA campus.

MORE TO THE
STORY

RIGHT VERSUS LEFT

On one side of the Charlottesville protests were people who came to attend the Unite the Right rally. The political term *right* can be confusing, since its meaning varies depending upon who's using it. At Charlottesville, the term referred to a set of beliefs and values supported by a mixture of extreme, violent, prowhite, antidiversity groups that often come under the heading of *alt-right*. That's short for *alternative right*.

Ordinary politics are often divided into right, which leans toward more traditional and conservative views, and left, which leans toward more progressive and liberal views. Alt-right groups are at the extreme conservative end of the spectrum. The members of most of those groups are what legal and political analysts have called white supremacists and nationalists. Alt-right groups believe the white race is superior to any other race.

On the opposing side in Charlottesville were people who see alt-right ideas and activities as evil and dangerous. Some of those people were members of Black Lives Matter and other prodiversity groups. Others were individual peace and diversity activists and supporters of anti-fascist, antihate causes. Some were described under the umbrella term *antifa*, short for *anti-fascists*. Some people have also called them the alt-left because they're opposed to everything alt-right.

Police watched the torchlit procession before the violence began on August 11, 2017.

He called the torchlit demonstration "a cowardly parade of hatred, bigotry, racism" and a "despicable display of visual intimidation."[5]

PREPARING FOR THE NEXT DAY

The disturbance ended with no major injuries or property damage. Still, city officials and law enforcement braced for the next day's Unite the Right rally. At noon on Saturday, thousands of protesters and counterprotesters would converge on Charlottesville's Emancipation Park. The stage was set for more confrontation and violence.

To understand what happened the next day and in the weeks that followed, it is necessary to understand the historical context. Like most civil strife, the Charlottesville protests were the result of a series of incidents, circumstances, events, and clashes—some of them stretching back more than 100 years. It is also necessary to understand the complicated set of issues and ideas that brought the various parties together in the first place.

"EVERYONE HAS A RIGHT UNDER THE FIRST AMENDMENT TO EXPRESS THEIR OPINION PEACEABLY, SO HERE'S MINE: NOT ONLY AS THE MAYOR OF CHARLOTTESVILLE, BUT AS A UVA FACULTY MEMBER AND ALUMNUS, I AM BEYOND DISGUSTED BY THIS UNSANCTIONED AND DESPICABLE DISPLAY OF VISUAL INTIMIDATION ON A COLLEGE CAMPUS."[6]

—CHARLOTTESVILLE MAYOR MIKE SIGNER, COMMENTING ON FACEBOOK CONCERNING THE AUGUST 11, 2017, PROTEST MARCH

CHAPTER TWO

STEPS TO
THE CONFLICT

Despite the disturbance the night before, the next morning, Saturday, August 12, Charlottesville city officials and police assured everyone the city was prepared for the day's scheduled rally at noon. The Virginia National Guard issued a statement that it would be there to "closely monitor the situation." Mayor Signer stated that he still intended "to make sure people can assemble and express themselves freely."[1]

Charlottesville residents were worried. A number of downtown businesses did not open for what would ordinarily have been a busy, profitable Saturday. Religious leaders held a sunrise service to pray for peace. Afterward, around 9:30 a.m., as a show of peace and unity, a group of approximately 20 ministers of

Charlottesville's Robert E. Lee statue was put up in 1924.

various faiths walked arm in arm to Emancipation Park where the Unite the Right rally was set to take place.[2]

Unite the Right's Facebook page stated that part of the rally's purpose was "to unify the right-wing against a totalitarian Communist crackdown, to speak out against displacement level immigration policies in the United States and Europe, and to affirm the right of Southerners and white people to organize for their interests just like any other group is able to do, free of persecution."[3] People who support extreme right causes often call those they oppose leftists or communists. They believe in the exclusion of all minorities and nationalities other than white Americans. They also believe any action that opens the door for diversity and interaction among races or nationalities is harmful.

Protesters and counterprotesters were already there, carrying signs, shouting, and chanting. Hundreds more, along with those in charge of keeping the peace, were elsewhere in the city, organizing and preparing for the day's event.

A BREWING STORM

This was not the first time Charlottesville had faced such turmoil. The issues and circumstances that led to this potentially explosive situation began long before August 2017. The first real sign of trouble brewing in Charlottesville occurred at a book talk in 2012 by Civil War historian Edward Ayers. After his presentation, Charlottesville City Council member Kristin Szakos asked Ayers if he thought it was time for her city to consider removing its Confederate statues. To many people, the monuments represented the racial division and injustice of slavery—the issue that divided the nation during the Civil War. Ayers said he favored exploring options other than removal, which satisfied Szakos.

Afterward, Szakos was surprised by other people's reactions to her seemingly innocent question. She began to receive hateful phone calls, letters, and even death threats. The issue of racial inequality was still controversial. Colleagues questioned her motives. Was she trying to start trouble? "I felt like I had put a stick in the ground and kind of ugly stuff bubbled up," she said later.[4] According to *New York Times* writer Jacey Fortin, the incident was a "local turning point."[5] It certainly opened the door for discussion in Charlottesville—and much more.

By that time, the vigorous debate over Confederate monuments and symbols had been going on for years. As early as 2000, South Carolina's legislature had passed the Heritage Act. The act called for the removal of the Confederate flag from the capitol dome. But the law still allowed the flag to be flown over the Confederate Soldiers' Monument on statehouse grounds. Some people thought the law didn't go far enough in mending the wounds inflicted by years of racial prejudice and injustice. In 2007, a school board in Florida refused the petition of residents who wanted to change the name of Nathan Bedford Forrest High School, where students were mostly African American. Nathan Bedford Forrest was a Confederate Army general and an early leader of the Ku Klux Klan (KKK). The school's name didn't change until 2014.

The debate concerning Confederate names and monuments started and continued primarily because

According to a 2015 poll, the majority of African Americans view the Confederate flag as a symbol of racism.

no one was able to agree on what the symbols meant.
Defenders of the Confederate symbols insisted that the
war was not fought over slavery and thus its symbols
were not racist. Others, including most historians, strongly
disagreed. But even those who argued that Confederate
monuments and symbols in public places were
inappropriate could not agree on what should be done
with them.

Led by Szakos, the Charlottesville City Council
unanimously voted in March 2015 to join at least six other
Virginia cities and no longer observe Lee–Jackson Day.
That Virginia state holiday commemorated two of the
Confederacy's most honored generals. "I think a lot of

our residents feel that doesn't represent them. It doesn't represent me," Szakos said prior to the vote.[6] The South Carolina Division of the Sons of Confederate Veterans bitterly objected. A statement on its website said the decision "flies in the face of genuine understanding, is purposely insulting and divisive, and is the kind of thinking that disrespects history, tradition, and heritage."[7] The post included the email addresses and phone numbers of Charlottesville's council members and mayor.

THE CHARLESTON SHOOTING AND THE CONFEDERATE FLAG

The debate over Confederate monuments reached a peak in 2015. Late on the evening of June 17, a young white man named Dylann Roof entered the Emanuel African Methodist Episcopal Church (AME)—which had a primarily black congregation—in downtown Charleston, South Carolina, and opened fire. Nine black men and women were killed, including AME's pastor Clementa C. Pinckney, who was also a South Carolina state senator.[8] Roof was later found guilty of multiple federal hate crimes and murder charges. He was sentenced to death.

Faith communities across the country prayed for AME after the deadly shooting.

The attack made headlines and shocked the nation, which was already reeling from news of other racially motivated shootings. Particularly troubling was Roof's confession that he had hoped his actions would ignite a bloody race war in the United States. Pictures found on his website showed him posing proudly with the Confederate flag in one hand and a gun in the other. Display of that symbol, in that context, struck a raw nerve for many people.

In South Carolina, it seemed intolerable to large numbers of people that the Confederate flag still flew prominently over government buildings and public places all over the nation. Just a month after the Charleston shooting, South Carolina governor Nikki Haley signed a bill that required the flag to be removed from capitol grounds and taken to a nearby Civil War museum.

Not everyone agreed. During debates on the issue, South Carolina Republican senator Lee Bright circulated a petition and sold bumper stickers that said, "Keep your hands off my flag."[9] Also, a June 2015 CNN poll revealed that 57 percent of Americans believed the Confederate flag was more a symbol of Southern pride than one of slavery and racism.[10]

"IN SOUTH CAROLINA WE HONOR TRADITION, WE HONOR HISTORY, WE HONOR HERITAGE, BUT THERE'S A PLACE FOR THAT FLAG AND THAT FLAG NEEDS TO BE IN A MUSEUM, WHERE WE WILL CONTINUE TO MAKE SURE PEOPLE WILL HONOR IT APPROPRIATELY. BUT THE STATEHOUSE, THAT'S AN AREA THAT BELONGS TO EVERYONE. AND NO ONE SHOULD DRIVE BY THE STATEHOUSE AND FEEL PAIN."[11]

—NIKKI HALEY, GOVERNOR OF SOUTH CAROLINA

Alabama law prohibits the removal or alteration of any Confederate monument. But in 2017, a week after the events in Charlottesville, the mayor of Birmingham, Alabama, William Bell, ordered the base of a Confederate monument in his city be covered with black panels. President Donald Trump quickly tweeted his objections.

"Sad to see the history and culture of our great country being ripped apart with the removal of our beautiful statues and monuments."[12] Bell saw the memorial in a different light. "It's a monument to segregation," he argued. "It's a monument to human bondage. It's a monument to sedition and the breakup of the United States of America."[13]

SPARKING CONVERSATIONS ACROSS THE NATION

As a direct reaction to the Charleston shooting, communities, cities, and states across the nation became embroiled in controversies over what to do about their own Confederate monuments and symbols. Statues and memorials to the Southern cause became points of protest.

In Charlottesville, days after the shooting, someone spray-painted "Black Lives Matter" on the base of the bronze statue of Lee.[14] Workers quickly removed the paint, but the intense feelings the words represented were not so easily erased. For many people, especially African Americans, a monument celebrating the Confederacy still

"AS A YOUNGER AFRICAN AMERICAN RESIDENT IN THIS CITY, I AM OFTEN EXPOSED TO DIFFERENT FORMS OF RACISM THAT ARE EMBEDDED IN THE HISTORY OF THE SOUTH AND PARTICULARLY THIS CITY. MY PEERS AND I FEEL STRONGLY ABOUT THE REMOVAL OF THE [ROBERT E. LEE] STATUE BECAUSE IT MAKES US FEEL UNCOMFORTABLE AND IT IS VERY OFFENSIVE."[16]

—CHARLOTTESVILLE HIGH SCHOOL STUDENT ZYAHNA BRYANT, IN A PETITION TO CITY COUNCIL SIGNED BY MORE THAN 300 SUPPORTERS

represented injustice, inequality, and hatred. Calls to remove the statue grew louder.

Six months after the Charleston killings, the city council in New Orleans, Louisiana, voted to remove its four Confederate statues. "They are not just innocent remembrances of a benign history," New Orleans mayor Mitch Landrieu said in 2017 when the last one came down. "These monuments celebrate a fictional, sanitized Confederacy ignoring the death, ignoring the enslavement, ignoring the terror that it actually stood for." Of Lee and other leaders he said, "They may have been warriors, but . . . they were not patriots."[15] City and regional leaders in Kentucky, Texas, Tennessee, and Florida also increased efforts to remove statues and monuments in their states.

In addition, a crowd of demonstrators in Durham, North Carolina, stormed the site of a Confederate monument outside the county courthouse on August 14, 2017. They used ropes to pull down the statue of a Southern soldier, then kicked it, stomped on it, and spat on it. Police did not try to stop the protesters. Other cities saw similar protests. In Louisville, Kentucky, a statue of a Confederate officer was splattered with orange paint. In Nashville, Tennessee, protesters draped a black jacket over the head of a statue of Nathan Bedford Forrest.

MONUMENTS TO A LOST CAUSE

According to historian Karen L. Cox, monuments honoring Confederate leaders and soldiers began to appear approximately 30 years after the Civil War ended. By the 1890s, most Southern states had enacted harsh legislation, known as Jim Crow laws, that severely restricted the rights of black citizens. "They were part of a campaign to paint the Southern cause in the Civil War as just and slavery as a benevolent institution," Cox said.[17]

A 2015 study conducted by the Southern Poverty Law Center (SPLC) found 718 Confederate monuments and statues on public property throughout the United States. Of these monuments, 551 were dedicated or built before

1950. More than 45 were dedicated or rededicated during the civil rights era. That period of struggle for black Americans is often described as occurring between the Supreme Court's school desegregation decision, known as *Brown v. Board of Education*, in 1954 and the assassination of Dr. Martin Luther King Jr. in 1968. The SPLC's survey also found 32 monuments and other symbols that were dedicated or rededicated in the years after 2000.[18]

The United Daughters of the Confederacy is primarily responsible for most of the Confederacy monuments. The group raised millions of dollars and erected hundreds of monuments across the country. The times and places in which most of the monuments were erected proves that they were "put up as explicit

"[THE CIVIL WAR] TESTED WHETHER OUR DEMOCRATIC INSTITUTIONS WERE STRONG ENOUGH TO WITHSTAND PROFOUND POLITICAL DIVISIONS. WILL THE CONSTITUTION AND THE INSTITUTIONS IT CREATED PROVE STRONG ENOUGH TO CARRY THE NATION THROUGH THE STORMY PERIOD OR WILL OUR DIVISIONS BREAK US APART? AMERICANS ASKED THIS QUESTION ABOUT THE STRUCTURAL INTEGRITY OF THEIR NATION IN 1861 AND THEY'RE ASKING IT AGAIN IN 2017."[19]

—JASON PHILLIPS, PROFESSOR OF CIVIL WAR STUDIES, WEST VIRGINIA UNIVERSITY

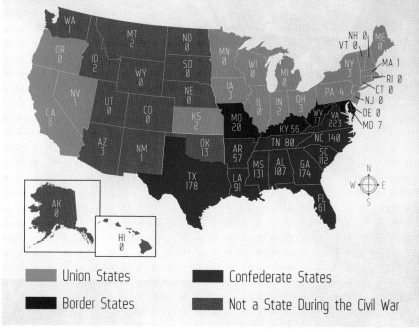

CONFEDERATE MONUMENTS AND SYMBOLS[21]

WA 1
MT 2
ND 0
OR 0
ID 2
SD 0
MN 0
WY 0
WI 0
MI 0
NY 3
NH 0
VT 0
ME 0
MA 1
RI 0
CT 0
NJ 0
DE 0
MD 7
NV 1
UT 0
NE 0
IA 3
IL 0
IN 2
OH 3
PA 4
WV 17
VA 223
CA 6
CO 0
KS 2
MO 20
KY 56
AZ 3
NM 1
OK 13
AR 57
TN 80
NC 140
MS 131
AL 107
GA 174
SC 112
TX 178
LA 91
FL 61
AK 0
HI 0

N W E S

Union States | Confederate States
Border States | Not a State During the Civil War

Formerly Confederate states have a significant number of Confederate monuments and symbols in public places compared with states that were not in the Confederacy.

symbols of white supremacy," according to Cox.[20] And many other historians agree.

Many of the monuments, such as Charlottesville's statue of Lee, were erected in the 1920s. According to historian Colin Woodward, it was a period somewhat like the modern-day United States—a turbulent time racially and politically. The KKK was enjoying unprecedented national popularity and its highest membership ever. White patriotism and antiblack and anti-immigrant feelings were powerful social undercurrents. The Republican Party was shifting from being a party that embraced the ideas of Abraham Lincoln, such as civil rights and economic restraint, and was rapidly becoming the party of Calvin Coolidge, embracing ideas of white privilege, big business, and unrestrained financial growth.

At the same time, in the former Confederate States, white supremacists were attempting to create a new vision of the South. This view, sometimes referred to as the Lost Cause, was based on the need to blame all of the South's postwar problems on the North. These white supremacists believed the North had stolen the Southern states' rights and heritage. The desire to reclaim that rosy, romantic version of the past drove much of the monument building that came after.

Not everyone who opposes the removal of Confederate statues supports alt-right or radical racist causes. Civil War author and historian Gary W. Gallagher believes that simply erasing objectionable statues and memorials from the public view is wrong. Instead, he favors "adding text that places monuments within the full sweep of how Americans have remembered the Civil War." He also supports the erecting of new monuments and the renaming of parks and streets to honor and recognize heroes of all races and cultures. Renaming Lee Park Emancipation Park was a good start. He suggests keeping the Confederate statue of Lee, "warts and all," and erecting nearby a monument to the US Colored Troops, groups of black soldiers who fought valiantly for the Union cause.[22]

THE ROBERT E. LEE STATUE

In March 2016, the Charlottesville City Council appointed a panel of citizens to study and discuss what to do about the Lee statue. Several months later, the committee report emphasized that it was important for the city government to act in a way that would clearly demonstrate its "rejection of the Jim Crow–era narratives that dominated when the statue was erected."[23]

CHARLOTTE'S 1929 MONUMENT CELEBRATION

A four-day celebration honoring Confederate veterans drew hundreds of thousands of people to the small community of Charlotte, North Carolina, in June 1929. A stone marker was erected in the public square to commemorate the event and the "valor of the Confederate soldier[s]" who fought "to preserve the Anglo-Saxon civilization of the South." According to William Barney, a history professor at the University of North Carolina, the words mean: "We're so proud of them for maintaining white supremacy."[24] In July 2015, someone smeared the monument with liquid cement, obscuring its objectionable words. The monument was cleaned. City leaders began discussing the removal of the monument.

Jason Kessler is a white nationalist who helped organize the Unite the Right rally.

In February 2017, the city council voted to remove the statue altogether.

Almost immediately, groups opposed to the move sued the city. Among them were the Sons of Confederate Veterans and Jason Kessler, a Charlottesville resident. A self-described white advocate and outspoken supporter of other alt-right causes, Kessler tried unsuccessfully to discredit and remove Charlottesville's African American vice mayor from office. He was among the most vocal opponents of moving the Lee statue.

The opposition's case was originally based on the assumption that moving the statue violated a 1904 Virginia law that said war memorials in the state could not be altered or removed. The city countered that the law was outdated and that the Lee statue was not a Civil War memorial. However, the opposition received a supportive ruling from a local judge in May 2017. Judge Richard Moore's decision was based on his belief that Virginia's monument law applies in that instance. The case would have to make its way through legal channels. In the meantime, the Lee statue had to remain where it was.

Leaders of groups that supported white supremacist causes around the country took note. National media coverage of Charlottesville's ongoing Confederate statue controversy had made Charlottesville the ideal place to stage a demonstration and get tons of free publicity. Kessler set about organizing an August 2017 Unite the Right rally that would draw people and groups from all over the country. "This entire community is a very far left community," he said in a statement that summarized the basic principles that unified what some were calling the alt-right. Kessler said the town and its leaders had "absorbed these cultural Marxist principles advocated in college towns across the country, about blaming white people for everything."[25]

Some people didn't want to wait until August. On Saturday, May 13, hundreds of alt-right protesters arrived in Charlottesville and converged on the city's parks. Alt-right activist and UVA graduate Richard Spencer spoke to several dozen supporters. His remarks were clearly aimed at city officials and those trying to do away with Confederate symbols. "We will never back down from the cowardly attacks on our people and our heritage," Spencer declared. "What brings us together is that we are white. We are a people. We will not be replaced!"[26] That night, Spencer led a group in a torchlit march to Emancipation Park. They rallied around the statue that had become the primary point of controversy.

The next night, counterprotesters staged a candlelit rally of their own in the park. At the foot of the Lee statue, speakers urged tolerance and peace. While the group sang hymns and chanted, several alt-right followers of Spencer showed up. Shouting and scuffling began. A police officer was injured and several people were arrested before the gathering ended.

On July 8, 2017, the KKK came to Charlottesville to stage a protest. This time, hundreds of anti-racism protesters turned out to meet them. Rallied by local religious leaders, they jeered and booed as dozens of KKK members, some wearing hoods and waving Confederate flags, marched through city streets. Some carried signs emblazoned with racial insults and anti-Jewish slogans. Escorted by police in riot gear, they gathered in a park called Justice Park. KKK leaders who tried to speak were shouted down by the counterprotesters who surrounded them. When shoving and fistfights broke out, police ended the disturbance with tear gas and began making arrests.

RICHARD SPENCER PREACHING HATRED

Richard Spencer coined the term *alt-right* and is a leader of the white nationalist movement in the United States. Spencer says he prefers to be called an identitarian, which is someone who identifies strictly with the white race. It is a group he claims is being dispossessed by other races. He also works tirelessly to bring about a "peaceful ethnic cleansing" in the United States. In other words, according to the SPLC, Spencer is just "a suit-and-tie version of the white supremacists of old." He was arrested in Hungary in 2014 and banned from 26 other European nations for three years for preaching racial hatred there.[28]

THE NEW FACE OF HATE

Protesters in Charlottesville included members of Vanguard America, Identity Evropa, the Traditionalist Worker Party, True Cascadia, the Proud Boys, the League of the South, and the National Socialist Movement. Many of these groups avoid old symbols of hate, such as skinned heads, swastikas, and hoods. Hate groups now recruit young white men who, until recently, were not politically active. Many of them are well educated, career oriented, and financially successful. But they're also darkly dissatisfied and angry. They believe minorities and immigrants are taking advantages that rightfully belong to white Americans and are eager to fight to stop them.

Afterward, some people who had experienced the turmoil criticized police. John Whitehead, founder of a civil liberties organization called the Rutherford Institute, had urged police before the rally to avoid using heavy-handed tactics and riot equipment. "What I saw . . . was not a community policing event," he said. "It was an armed police state. It's not a good image to portray around the nation." Charlottesville's chief of police, Al Thomas, refused to comment on accusations that police had overreacted. He said only that he and city leaders would "assess our successes and shortcomings" from the July rally.[29] Truly assessing and understanding exactly what happened that day and in the days that followed required a much longer look back at specific historic events and circumstances at the very roots of the United States' racial divide.

Al Thomas was criticized for how he handled the situation in Charlottesville.

FROM THE
HEADLINES

THE FACE OF A MOVEMENT

A week after the Charleston church shooting, activist Bree Newsome decided she had to make a bold statement. In the early morning of June 27, 2015, she climbed the 30-foot (9 m) flagpole near the capitol in Columbia, South Carolina, and took down the Confederate flag. "I removed the flag not only in defiance of those who enslaved my ancestors in the southern United States," Newsome wrote later, "but also in defiance of the oppression that continues against black people globally in 2015."[30]

Newsome was quickly arrested and the flag replaced. But photos and video of Newsome hanging from the pole, holding the flag in triumph, went viral on social media. Such bold gestures do sometimes sway public opinion. The president of the North Carolina branch of the National Association for the Advancement of Colored People, Rev. Dr. William J. Barber II, compared Newsome's actions to those of civil rights pioneer Rosa Parks.

Bree Newsome took down the Confederate flag as people watched from below.

CHAPTER THREE

LOOKING
BACK

What exactly motivated Unite the Right
protesters in Charlottesville? What drove them
to shout racial slurs and carry "White lives
matter" signs? As journalist Ryan Cooper said, "White
terror today grows up the frame of a historical trellis
well over 150 years old."[1] Most historians believe that
much of today's postslavery racial strife may be traced
directly to the period after the Civil War known as
Reconstruction. During that relatively short period, the
federal government attempted to help Southern states
devastated by the war rebuild and rejoin the Union.
One important part of this project was an effort to assist
formerly enslaved people through education and other

The KKK terrorized black Americans for decades. The group is still
around in more than a dozen states.

programs to become free, independent, and equal citizens and partners in the reformation of the Union.

Unfortunately, as history shows, racial prejudice undercut and stopped the humanitarian project before it had time to do much good. Political indifference and social undercurrents doomed Reconstruction almost from the beginning. Money and military protection were soon withdrawn from the South. Millions of former slaves were left to face poverty and the rage of white Southerners still stinging from the loss of the war and their most treasured cultural and economic institution: slavery. White supremacist organizations such as the KKK organized and began a campaign of terror and intimidation aimed at black people that lasted well into the 1900s.

THE HAMBURG MASSACRE

Some black citizens tried to stand up against mob violence during Reconstruction. In 1876, in Hamburg, South Carolina, African Americans formed an armed militia to protect themselves and their families from attacks by rampaging gangs of white supremacists. In response, a vicious white paramilitary group called the Red Shirts attacked Hamburg in large numbers. They terrorized the black population and executed some of the militia members. The attack basically ended black resistance in South Carolina. Similar attacks in other places were equally bloody and repressive.

VIOLENCE
AND DEMONSTRATIONS

Instead of rising from slavery, millions of African Americans were essentially reenslaved by black codes. These laws, enacted by most Southern states in the last decades of the 1800s, prevented blacks from voting, owning property, or earning a decent living. The constant threat of violence made it nearly impossible for black people to improve their lives.

Perhaps the most horrific tool of racial oppression used against blacks in the South and elsewhere during that time was lynching. This term refers to a wide range of racially motivated torture and killing. These unspeakable acts of violence were most often performed in public and routinely included shootings, hangings, burnings,

JEFFERSON'S CONTROVERSIAL PAST

On September 12, 2017, approximately 40 UVA students gathered on the university campus to cover the statue of Jefferson with black tarps. They were there to call attention to the fact that Jefferson, the founder of the school, was also a slaveholder. They carried signs reading "End Hate Now," "Black Lives Matter," and "TJ was a racist and rapist."[2] The latter sign refers to the fact that Jefferson fathered at least six children of Sally Hemings, who was his slave and therefore had no real choice in the matter. UVA president Teresa Sullivan acknowledged those troubling facts but also felt that the students were "desecrating ground that many of us consider sacred." She also pointed out the university's efforts to honor the contribution of the slaves who "not only built its buildings, but also served in a wide variety of capacities for UVA's first 50 years of existence."[3]

MORE TO THE
STORY

"IMPOSSIBLE TO REMAIN SILENT"

Many people believe that violence against African Americans after the Civil War was confined to the South. But lynchings took place in many parts of the country. A Duluth, Minnesota, monument erected in 2003 is one of a growing number of permanent public displays that graphically illustrate that fact. The memorial commemorates the public executions of Elmer Jackson, Elias Clayton, and Isaac McGhie in June 1920 in Duluth. The three young black men had been falsely accused of assaulting a white woman. A mob of some 10,000 people watched as the men were hung from public utility poles.

The memorial was built at the street corner site of the lynching at a cost of $267,000—raised from private donations. A local woman anonymously gave $10,000.[4] A relative of hers had been working at the jail the night of the killing and had done nothing to stop it. He'd grieved until the day he died, she said.

Engraved across the top of the monument in large letters are the words first spoken by British statesman Edmund Burke in 1789 but still relevant in 2003: "An event has happened upon which it is difficult to speak and impossible to remain silent."[5]

rapes, and mutilations. In 2017, the Equal Justice Initiative (EJI), a nonprofit civil rights organization, published a list of known lynching incidents in the United States between the end of Reconstruction in 1877 and 1950. The list was compiled after years of research and documents 3,959 incidents of what the EJI calls "systematic domestic terrorism."[6]

"WHITE SUPREMACISTS AND NEO-NAZIS CAME OUT IN FORCE TO DEFEND A CONFEDERATE STATUE. YET, THE LESSON TO TAKE FROM CHARLOTTESVILLE IS NOT THAT THOSE IDEAS PERSIST, BUT THAT THEY ARE BEING SHARPLY AND QUICKLY REBUKED BY A MORAL MAJORITY. UNLIKE TIMES OF THE PAST, THERE IS NO MAINSTREAM CONSTITUENCY WILLING TO OVERTLY DEFEND RACISM."[7]

—DEREK W. BLACK, PROFESSOR OF LAW, UNIVERSITY OF SOUTH CAROLINA

Demonstrations, protests, and riots that took place during the civil rights movement of the 1960s were direct reactions by African Americans to years of social, political, and economic repression. The Civil Rights and Voting Rights Acts of 1964 and 1965 were the hard-won prizes of these struggles. These historic pieces of legislation dismantled Jim Crow segregation and removed barriers that had prevented African Americans from voting in many places. But the KKK and other groups, such as the National Socialist Movement and Aryan Nations, did not go away.

In the modern-day United States, as the protests in Charlottesville clearly show, racist groups are still active. Their goal is the same as it was in 1865 and 1965—to bar people of certain races, religions, nationalities, and gender identities from the constitutional rights afforded to all American citizens. They work hard to achieve that goal, and those who oppose them work equally as hard to stop them.

"CONGRESS SHALL MAKE NO LAW RESPECTING AN ESTABLISHMENT OF RELIGION, OR PROHIBITING THE FREE EXERCISE THEREOF; OR ABRIDGING THE FREEDOM OF SPEECH, OR OF THE PRESS; OR THE RIGHT OF THE PEOPLE PEACEABLY TO ASSEMBLE, AND TO PETITION THE GOVERNMENT FOR A REDRESS OF GRIEVANCES."[8]

—**FIRST AMENDMENT TO THE CONSTITUTION**

Black Lives Matter members participated in the Charlottesville rally. The organization aims to improve black people's lives.

FROM THE
HEADLINES

RIGHTING THE WRONGS OF HISTORY?

Attempts by cities and states to adjust traditional history have involved more than just statues. In the 1990s, the New Orleans Parish School District in Louisiana changed the names of some schools originally named for Confederate leaders. In 2017, officials in Houston, Texas, changed the names of one street and some schools—all originally named after people with Confederate connections.

It is not always about the Civil War and racial wrongs, either. In San Francisco, California, gender is the issue. Efforts there are underway to convince city leaders to add statues and streets honoring historically important women. It is part of a nationwide movement to balance the historical ledger already overflowing with historical monuments dedicated to male leaders and achievers. Joan Bradley Wages, president of the National Women's History Museum in Washington, DC, speaks for the movement. She notes that not talking about historical women leads people to believe that women haven't played a role in building the United States.

New Orleans removed its statue of Robert E. Lee in 2017.

CHAPTER FOUR

THE
PROTEST

On August 12, 2017, counterprotesters arriving at Emancipation Park around eight o'clock in the morning found large numbers of alt-right protesters already there. The alt-right protesters shouted racist slogans and waved Confederate flags and banners emblazoned with swastikas. Although not all of them had arrived yet, one reporter estimated the alt-right forces in Charlottesville that day were between 1,000 and 1,500 people.[1]

Some demonstrators wore military-style clothing, shields, body armor, and helmets. Among the mix were a number of self-appointed and heavily armed civilian militias. They told police, who were watching the proceedings from two sides of the park, that they

Counterprotesters marched into Emancipation Park to show their displeasure with the alt-right.

"IS [THE ARMED INDIVIDUAL] SOMEONE WHO ANSWERS TO A DEMOCRATICALLY-ELECTED OFFICIAL, OR IS IT WHOEVER WANTS TO CLAIM THEMSELVES TO BE A MILITIA, AND, BECAUSE OF OUR LAX GUN LAWS, ARMS THEMSELVES TO THE TEETH TO MAKE THEM INDISTINGUISHABLE FROM REAL PUBLIC SAFETY PEOPLE? IT LEAVES LAW ENFORCEMENT FEELING CONSTRAINED ABOUT HOW ASSERTIVE THEY CAN BE TO TAKE CONTROL OF A SITUATION NOT KNOWING IF THIS GROUP IS GOING TO TURN ON THEM."[2]

—DANIEL WEBSTER, DIRECTOR OF THE CENTER FOR GUN POLICY AND RESEARCH AT JOHNS HOPKINS UNIVERSITY

were there to help them keep order. That didn't make many people, especially the police, feel any safer.

Counterprotesters were also there in large numbers. Exact numbers of those opposing the Unite the Right rally were harder to estimate. Some were local residents, people who mostly weren't carrying signs or flags or wearing specific emblems or distinctive clothing. Others were a somewhat loosely organized mixture of representatives from various anti-fascist and anti-racist organizations, as well as individual peace and civil rights activists and religious leaders.

Much more organized and aggressive counterprotesters were also present. These were people the media had labeled *antifa*—short for *anti-fascists*. Most of them had come to Charlottesville with one purpose: to match the alt-right's threatening show of force with physical intimidation of their own.

With some people on both sides spoiling for a fight, it didn't take long that morning for shouting and name-calling to escalate into something more. As more people began to converge on Emancipation Park from all directions, pushing and jostling soon turned into spitting, cursing, and punching.

Quickly, just as they had the night before, things spun wildly out of control. By nine o'clock in the morning, the battle was on. Protesters began to attack and punch one another. Choking mace and pepper spray filled the air. A few agitators threw balloons filled with urine, bleach, and other foul-smelling substances. Demonstrators on both sides fought, individually and in small groups, using fists, flagpoles, rocks, clubs, and other makeshift weapons.

FIGHTING WORDS

The First Amendment to the US Constitution guarantees citizens the right to publicly assemble, argue, and protest. But what about shouting hateful words intended specifically to provoke a fight? In the 1942 case of *Chaplinsky v. New Hampshire*, the Supreme Court ruled that free speech rights do not extend to "fighting words." The court defined that kind of speech as words "which by their very utterance inflict injury or tend to incite an immediate breach of the peace."[3] Several legal experts studied and analyzed specific language used by protesters in Charlottesville. They found that in several cases protesters on both sides did cross the line that separates protected speech from fighting words.

THE FIGHTING INTENSIFIES

As fighting around Emancipation Park intensified, police and members of the Virginia National Guard watched the conflict unfolding and appeared to do nothing to stop it. They had blocked two sides of the park, but not the third. As the fighting continued and escalated, the conflict eventually spilled from the park and out onto Market Street.

At around 11 o'clock in the morning, several dozen alt-right protesters appeared on Market Street, marching in tight formation. Antifa counterprotesters quickly assembled, forming a line across the street, intentionally blocking the alt-right protesters from advancing. Roaring with rage, the two groups charged together and began beating one another with fists and clubs and spraying

FREE SPEECH IN BOSTON

One week after the Charlottesville protests, several dozen alt-right supporters held a rally in the Boston Common in Massachusetts. The speakers wanted to voice their claims that their right to free speech had been violated in Charlottesville and elsewhere. But their words were drowned out by shouts from tens of thousands of people who packed the streets around the park. Police arrested 33 people for disorderly conduct and assaults, approximately the same number as in Charlottesville. Still, Boston mayor Marty Walsh said, "It's clear today that Boston stood for peace and love, not bigotry and hate."[4]

Alt-right protesters and counterprotesters clashed during the rally.

chemical irritants. Counterprotesters from various vantage points hurled curses and balloons filled with paint or ink.

Other conflicts, large and small, seemed to be going on everywhere one looked. Injured, bloodied people, many of them onlookers and not part of either side, approached police and begged for help.

At 11:20 a.m., police began to strap on riot gear and prepared to clear Emancipation Park. City and state security officials had decided the situation was far too chaotic to allow the noon Unite the Right rally to take place. People at the park were ordered to leave immediately. After a brief standoff between alt-right protesters and police, some alt-right protesters moved from Emancipation Park to McIntire Park a short distance away. There, the smaller crowd gathered to listen to some of the speakers who had been scheduled for the Unite the Right event. Though anti-fascist protesters heckled the gathering, police kept them at a distance to lessen the chance of further flare-ups.

Unite the Right leaders were not pleased with the sudden turn of events. McIntire Park was the place the city had asked organizers to hold the rally in the first place. They had objected then because the Lee statue was integral to their purpose and message. The originally stated reason for the rally, after all, was to protest the city's planned removal of that statue from Emancipation Park.

A DEADLY OUTCOME

As the protest broke up, social media hummed as both sides began to claim victory and cast blame on the other side for starting the violence. Ugly images of the fighting and more name-calling flooded Facebook pages. As bad as it appeared, city officials mostly heaved a sigh of relief. It appeared the whole dreadful thing was over, without any serious injuries or property damage done.

After the cancellation of the Unite the Right rally, anti-racist protesters had mostly moved farther downtown toward the courthouse. Pedestrians clogged the streets, some of which had been barricaded to prevent car traffic. A large concentration of people had gathered at the intersection of Fourth Street Southeast and Water Street.

Shortly after one o'clock in the afternoon, a silver-gray car appeared suddenly, traveling quickly on Fourth Street Southeast, heading straight for the crowd of people. Videos and photos taken by media professionals and bystanders from a variety of angles recorded the scene. The screech of tires and a thud could be heard on the videos as the car

WHITE NATIONALISM AND THE ALT-RIGHT

White supremacists believe the white race is superior to all others. White nationalists, sometimes called white separatists, believe that, too. But they take it a step further. In order to preserve their culture, as one white nationalist once said, the white race should have a nation to itself. That land must be free of Muslims, Jews, and Africans and other people of color. In many ways, alt-right and white nationalism mean about the same thing, according to the SPLC. The SPLC notes that both feature "concern over white identity, belief that Western civilization is crumbling, that liberal democracy has failed, and that a symptom of this failure is multiculturalism."[5]

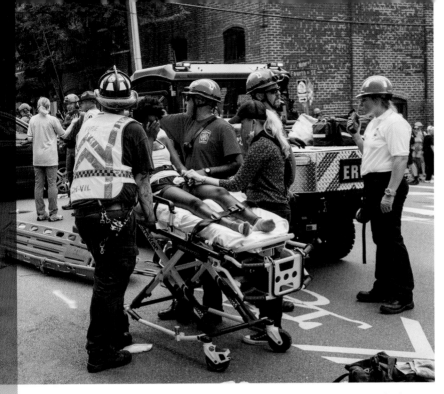

First responders helped people who were injured after a car crashed into a crowd on August 12.

struck people before crashing into another vehicle. Bodies flew through the air. People screamed and there was panic as the car reversed and sped backward for several blocks. People began to leap frantically out of the car's path as the car and its crumpled front bumper sped away.

It all happened in seconds. People rushed to help those who'd been struck. Heather Heyer, a 32-year-old paralegal from Charlottesville, and at least 19 others were taken to a nearby hospital.[6] Heyer died there of her injuries. An impromptu memorial appeared on Fourth Street Southeast with a pile of flowers and pictures of

Heyer. Friends and family members later stated that Heyer had been committed to peace and unity and believed in standing up against anyone who preached hatred and injustice.

News of the attack spread quickly through Twitter. While some alt-right organizers shared crude jokes and self-congratulations over the death online, police were busy tracking down the perpetrator. They quickly located the damaged car. Soon after, they arrested the driver. His name was James Fields. He was an Ohio resident with a history of neo-Nazi and white supremacist activities. Photos emerged later showing Fields in Charlottesville marching with alt-right protesters earlier in the day.

Fields faced a number of charges, including one count of first-degree murder. In June 2018, Fields was also charged with federal hate crimes for his actions in Charlottesville. Hate crimes are motivated by hostility

"WE THOUGHT, 'WHAT WOULD HEATHER DO?' HEATHER WOULD GO HARDER. SO THAT'S WHAT WE'RE GOING TO DO. WE'RE GOING TO PREACH LOVE. WE'RE GOING TO PREACH EQUALITY, AND HEATHER'S DEATH WON'T BE IN VAIN."[7]

—MARISSA BLAIR, FRIEND OF HEATHER HEYER

toward a person based on things such as his or her race, gender, religion, or sexual orientation. The FBI and US Department of Justice officials reported that they intended to open a civil rights investigation into the violence that happened in Charlottesville. Any evidence that Fields or others had planned the attack before coming to Charlottesville from Ohio would elevate the charges substantially.

"The violence and deaths in Charlottesville strike at the heart of American law and justice," US attorney general Jeff Sessions said shortly after Fields's arrest. "When such actions arise from racial bigotry and hatred, they betray our core values and cannot be tolerated. Justice will prevail."[8]

People placed flowers on the Charlottesville sidewalk where Heather Heyer was fatally injured.

CHAPTER FIVE

POLICE AND
THE PROTEST

P olice and city officials pointed out that the small space and location of Emancipation Park where the Unite the Right rally was to be held contributed to the chaos. In fact, they recognized early on that having a rally there could turn into a public-safety issue. Because of this, the city denied Unite the Right's original permit request, recommending instead the larger McIntire Park across town, where law enforcement could better control and separate the two opposing sides.

But the night before the rally, the American Civil Liberties Union (ACLU) filed a lawsuit on behalf of Kessler's group. The suit claimed that moving the rally to another place violated Kessler's and others'

Many people criticized how police handled the Unite the Right rally.

constitutional rights to free speech and assembly. The planned removal of the Lee statue in Emancipation Park was precisely the issue Unite the Right demonstrators were there to protest. That specific park and statue were symbolically vital to the presentation of their message, organizers said. And, on Friday evening, August 11, US district judge Glen E. Conrad ruled in favor of Kessler and Unite the Right. The city government could not deny the constitutional rights of Kessler and others to speak in a public place.

Afterward, Josh Blackman, an associate professor at the South Texas College of Law in Houston, observed that the city messed up its chance to bar Unite the Right protesters. Initially, the Charlottesville City Council had granted Kessler's permit application along with those of counterprotesters.

THE FIRST AMENDMENT IN ACTION

Judge Conrad ruled that the decision to allow Unite the Right's permit to meet in Charlottesville was based solely on the US Constitution. Under the First Amendment, he said, "a municipal government . . . has no power to restrict expression because of its message, its ideas, its subject matter, or its content." He also stated that the city had failed to prove that anyone would "suffer irreparable harm" as a result of Unite the Right's assembly or speech. He dismissed the city's argument that the huge crowds that were expected in the city would seriously endanger anyone's life. "There is no evidence to support the notion that many thousands of individuals are likely to attend the demonstration," he said.[1]

Later, they moved to revoke Kessler's permit to protest in the city. But at that time they failed to also revoke those of the counterprotesters. In his ruling, Conrad specifically mentioned that fact. He used it as evidence that city leaders were biased against Kessler's message and favored that of the counterprotesters. The judge also noted that city leaders' posts on social media showed that they were against Kessler's viewpoint. Caught in that legal bind, the city had no choice but to allow the rally to take place under less-than-secure circumstances.

RESPONSE TO THE VIOLENCE

After the Charlottesville protests, one of the few things protesters and counterprotesters agreed on was the apparent inaction of police. "There was no police presence," one Charlottesville resident said. "We were watching people punch each other. People were bleeding all the while police were inside of barricades at the park, watching. It was essentially just brawling on the street and community members trying to protect each other."[2]

Kessler went even further. He said police actually provoked and encouraged violence by failing to separate

WERE POLICE INTIMIDATED?

The line of camouflage-clothed militia members carrying assault rifles outside of Emancipation Park was a concern for police in Charlottesville. Even after the militia members identified themselves as a private paramilitary group legally carrying weapons, police were still concerned. Governor Terry McAuliffe noted after the protests that these militia members had better gear than the police. How much that firepower kept police officers from doing their job is a matter of debate. But some observers did believe the police looked intimidated by the protesters' armed display of weapons, though Thomas denied that this was the case.

members of the rally from counterprotesters. He said his group had worked with police months before the rally and they had agreed on a plan for maintaining safety. "They stood down and did not follow through with the agreed-upon security arrangements," Kessler wrote in a statement later.[3] He added that police were "under-equipped for the situation, they stood idly by when violent counter-protesters attacked participants of our rally, and then they forced our demonstrators out of Lee Park and into a melee with Antifa."[4]

Chief Thomas had a different viewpoint. He said it was Kessler and his overenthusiastic alt-right protesters who had not followed the preexisting plan. Thomas noted that police planned to allow protesters in at one section of the park, but protesters entered the park through various locations. Thomas said that the chaotic and totally unexpected mixing and mingling of protesters and counterprotesters made it impossible for police to form a noncombat buffer zone between the two groups. There simply was no time or space for police to maneuver.

The already bad situation worsened as the day continued. Combative crowds began to spread outward from cramped Emancipation Park. Thomas described the challenge that faced his officers once the brawling moved out onto the streets. He noted that his forces were spread thin. Corinne Geller, a spokesperson for the Virginia State Police, believed it was exactly this rapid spread of the crowds that led people to think police weren't doing anything to control the situation. A large number of police were actually stationed all over Charlottesville, she said. Many state and local officers were

A CLEAR AND PRESENT DANGER?

In the 1919 case *Schenck v. United States*, the Supreme Court ruled that civil authorities can restrict a person's right to free speech if that speech brings about danger and could hurt society. ACLU director Claire Gastañaga was referring to that case when she said that Charlottesville leaders had failed to present proper evidence that would have allowed the judge to declare a legal "imposition of prior restraint on free speech."[5] Such evidence might have allowed the change of venue to the larger park to take place.

indeed standing and watching, but there were many other officers who stepped in when they saw conflict break out, Geller said.

Other people unofficially voiced their opinion that city officials in the days before the protests might have ordered police to step aside and not interfere if things grew violent. Some people recalled how quickly police donned riot gear and fired tear gas during the KKK disturbance in July. They wondered if criticism leveled at state and local police then might have led police to adopt a less forceful approach during the August protests. Thomas denied those rumors, but the ideas persisted.

In late 2017, the city hired a former federal prosecutor to conduct a review into Thomas's response to the rally. In December 2017, Thomas retired after receiving a negative review. In 2018, Charlottesville hired RaShall M. Brackney as the

LIVES ON THE LINE FOR FREE SPEECH

Adding to the tragedy in Charlottesville was the crash of a state police helicopter not far from town later in the afternoon. Two veteran officers—Jay Cullen and Berke Bates—died in the accident. The officers in the aircraft were monitoring vehicle traffic and the movements of crowds in and around the city. The crash was not a direct result of violence on the ground. Still, officials noted, the officers would not have been in the air had it not been for circumstances on the ground.

Fighting broke out in front of the Charlottesville police station on August 12.

next police chief. Brackney was the first African American woman to hold this position in the Charlottesville Police Department.

STATE OF EMERGENCY

Afterward, no one said that police were slow to act once a state of emergency was declared. That term refers to a special governmental declaration that alerts citizens to change their normal behavior and that orders law enforcement and other agencies to begin more active and coordinated efforts to protect people and property.

Brian Moran, Virginia's secretary of public safety and homeland security, was watching events from the sixth floor of a downtown bank building. As soon as he saw that

MORE TO THE
STORY

UNREGULATED MILITIAS

The difficulty armed private militias present to law enforcement was very much on display in Charlottesville. One independent militia was the self-proclaimed Pennsylvania Light Foot Militia. The group said it was in town to defend free speech but vowed to protect the rights of everyone in the conflict. Another militia was anything but neutral. Members of the Redneck Revolt—a leftist, anti-racist, anti-capitalist militia—were there strictly to defend counterprotesters. Most members of legitimate military and law enforcement agree that during out-of-control demonstrations, the presence of unregulated militias creates unnecessary confusion about who's in charge.

One danger is that during an emergency, people may expect private militias to do things they're not legally permitted to do. Leaders of the Virginia National Guard became concerned about that very thing in Charlottesville. They didn't want people to confuse members of the National Guard with members of private militias. At 12:04 p.m. that day, after a state of emergency was declared, the state National Guard tweeted a message warning people to look for the distinct patches the state militia members wore on their uniforms.

One private militia group, the Three Percenters, has voluntarily resigned from engaging in protests like Charlottesville in the future. The group noted that it doesn't want the media to paint it in a negative light. Some experts think other private militias may follow suit. Members want to separate themselves from more radical and violent groups intent on anti-government actions. Some militias have vowed to blow up government buildings and even assassinate public officials.

Police eventually began making arrests, but many people thought they acted too late.

things were out of control, around 11:20 a.m., he phoned Governor Terry McAuliffe, who immediately declared a state of emergency. Officers in riot gear and National Guard troops quickly cleared Emancipation Park and established order.

In the days following the protests, city and state officials continued to blame alt-right organizers and protesters for the violence. They also admitted things like this could be handled differently. "We have to do a better job working with the judiciary. They need to listen to local city officials," McAuliffe said. "I am angry that this was not moved to McIntire Park where the city of Charlottesville requested."[6]

CHAPTER SIX

GUNS IN
THE STREETS

During the protests, the media and Charlottesville residents watched with growing alarm as the brutal spectacle unfolded. *New York Times* reporter Hawes Spencer described how he and others had to duck and dodge the "constant stream of projectiles whizzing by our faces" and how "the air was filled with the sounds of fists and sticks against flesh."[1]

The fact that so many protesters brandished pistols and semiautomatic rifles only added to people's sense of dread that something terrible could happen at any moment. Yet Virginia and Charlottesville gun laws allow civilians to openly carry weapons. Legally, there was very little police could do unless people actually started firing their weapons.

Protesters from each side were angry during the Unite the Right rally.

CHARLOTTESVILLE 3.0

On October 7, 2017, white nationalists once again protested in Charlottesville. Calling it Charlottesville 3.0, approximately 50 protesters arrived by bus without apparent notice beforehand. They met, carrying torches, around the tarp-covered statue of Lee in Emancipation Park for approximately ten minutes, then quickly left. Spencer, the group's leader, tweeted afterward, "We came, we triggered, we left. We did an in-and-out flash mob. We're going to do it again."[3] The surprise prompted the city to form a legal task force to explore ways to bar future visits by hate groups. The city said it wanted to explore ways to ban guns from public demonstrations as well.

The Second Amendment to the US Constitution deals with the right to bear arms. The problem, according to Geoffrey R. Stone, a law professor at the University of Chicago, is the amendment's vague and confusing wording. Legal scholars have debated its actual meaning for years.

The debate centers on the fact that the Second Amendment is composed of two clauses. The first, a dependent clause, says, "A well regulated Militia, being necessary to the security of a free State." The second, an independent clause, "the right of the people to keep and bear Arms shall not be infringed," completes the statement.[2] The last word, *infringed*, means broken, taken away, or trespassed upon. People in favor of strict gun control believe the first clause governs the second. Only state militias should be allowed to own and carry firearms.

Those who oppose gun control think the second clause is the only one that matters. Any individual should have the right to bear arms.

The US Supreme Court attempted to clarify things in 2008, in the case of *District of Columbia v. Heller*. It ruled in favor of the second clause. Justice Antonin Scalia stated in his majority opinion that the phrase "the people" in the Constitution referred not only to members of the state militia but to all citizens. The Second Amendment, he wrote, "surely elevates above all other interests the right of law-abiding, responsible citizens to use arms in defense of hearth and home."[4]

However, the court did add that its interpretation should not prevent cities, states, or the federal government from restricting when and where people should be allowed to carry guns. And that has happened

FIVE LITTLE WORDS

Retired Supreme Court Justice John Paul Stevens has called the ever-growing number of guns in private hands a tragedy in the United States. He blames the free access and public display of firearms by anyone, no matter how sane or careful, "a misinterpretation of the Second Amendment." The situation could be remedied, he says, by the addition of five simple words to the amendment—"when serving in the militia." That would at least eliminate "one mistaken argument" over what he believes is "the original intent" of the Second Amendment: standing armies in defense of the nation should have free access to deadly weapons, not just any individual who wants one.[5]

"THE CRITICAL QUESTION IS HOW TO PROTECT PEOPLES' FREE SPEECH IN THE PRESENCE OF ARMED OPPONENTS. THE GUN LOBBY HAS WORKED TO PASS LAWS IN VIRGINIA AND OTHER STATES TO PREVENT LOCAL GOVERNMENTS FROM PASSING RESTRICTIONS ON OPEN CARRY. BUT LEGAL RESEARCHERS POINT TO ELEMENTS IN STATE LAWS AND SUPREME COURT DECISIONS SAYING THAT THE RIGHT TO BEAR ARMS IN PUBLIC IS NOT ABSOLUTE AND MUST STOP SHORT OF INDUCING FEAR IN OTHERS."[7]

—*NEW YORK TIMES* EDITORIAL BOARD

in some places. For instance, California has some of the most restrictive gun laws in the nation, including a ban on the private ownership of assault rifles. However, most other states have no laws that keep people from openly carrying guns in public places.

LIMITING CITIZENS' RIGHTS

The debate over gun control has grown into one of the most divisive issues in the nation. A 2017 Pew Research Center survey showed that attitudes about guns and gun control have changed a great deal since 2000. Fifty-one percent of people polled said they wanted more gun control, while 47 percent said they favored actions by government that gave people more gun rights. In 2000, approximately 75 percent of all those surveyed said they wanted more gun control measures.[6]

But the issue in regard to what happened in Charlottesville was less about gun ownership, the right to bear arms, or even the right to openly carry guns. It was more about regulating under what conditions and circumstances people can be forbidden from carrying loaded weapons.

John Feinblatt, a gun control activist, believes that situations like those in Charlottesville make clear just

John Feinblatt is the president of Everytown for Gun Safety, which is a nonprofit organization that pushes for gun control.

how dangerous things can become when hundreds of angry people are in open, public confrontation, verbally and physically battling one another. He believes the odds that someone might suddenly snap and open fire skyrocket in those situations.

Carrying guns at a public demonstration has never been a constitutionally protected right, Feinblatt says. "According to the framers," he wrote in a 2017 *New York Times* editorial piece, "the First Amendment protected the right to 'peaceably'—not violently or threateningly—assemble." People who came to Charlottesville openly carrying firearms, Feinblatt said, "were neither conveying a nonviolent political message, nor engaged in self-defense nor protecting hearth and home." Their clear intent was "to intimidate and terrify protesters and the police."[8]

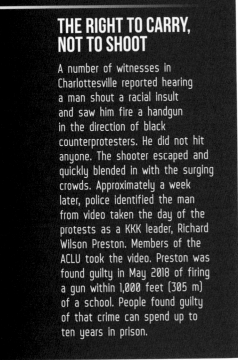

THE RIGHT TO CARRY, NOT TO SHOOT

A number of witnesses in Charlottesville reported hearing a man shout a racial insult and saw him fire a handgun in the direction of black counterprotesters. He did not hit anyone. The shooter escaped and quickly blended in with the surging crowds. Approximately a week later, police identified the man from video taken the day of the protests as a KKK leader, Richard Wilson Preston. Members of the ACLU took the video. Preston was found guilty in May 2018 of firing a gun within 1,000 feet (305 m) of a school. People found guilty of that crime can spend up to ten years in prison.

The Supreme Court ruled on a similar case in 1886 known as *Presser v. Illinois*. That case involved an incident during which Herman Presser, without a legal permit, led a large group of heavily armed militia members down the streets of Chicago. The court ruled that the state law in place at that time clearly forbade groups of men to walk around with guns unless they were given special permission. For the US Founding Fathers, Feinblatt stated, such a law was needed to keep people safe, and it still is today.

The organizers of the Unite the Right rally in Charlottesville understood that many attendees would bring guns. They didn't discourage it. In fact, many people thought it was a good idea. In the weeks prior to the event, discussions in alt-right chat rooms and on white supremacist websites discussed the issue of optics. The term referred to how rally participants hoped to appear to the media and outsiders watching the event. Organizers hoped the sight of people toting guns would make them look powerful. They also thought it might make them and their cause more attractive to the National Rifle Association and other gun-supporting organizations.

Wayne LaPierre is the executive vice president of the National Rifle
Association. This organization supports gun rights.

At the same time, organizers knew violence was likely, and they warned those carrying guns against firing their weapons. Appearing careless or out of control were things they hoped to avoid. One organizer—whose gender is unknown—wrote that they encouraged people to bring guns but only use the weapons in self-defense.

The debate over who should have the right to carry guns during public demonstrations is not a new one. Law enforcement officials, by and large, believe that ordinary citizens with guns only divert their attention from the real threat. Police officers often ask how they should know whether the person they see carrying a weapon in public has defense or offense in mind. Police in states with open carry laws face the dilemma frequently. Citizens report someone with a gun on the street or in a store. They call the police, who then face the challenge of determining whether the individual is a threat.

"THE PRESENCE OF MANY GUNS, PARTICULARLY THE SORT THAT CAN KILL MANY PEOPLE IN VERY LITTLE TIME, MAY DISSUADE LAW ENFORCEMENT FROM STEPPING IN WHEN A PROTEST GETS OUT OF HAND. THE RESULT IS AN ALARMING FORM OF CENSORSHIP: NONVIOLENT DEMONSTRATORS LOSE THEIR RIGHT TO ASSEMBLE AND EXPRESS THEIR IDEAS BECAUSE THE POLICE ARE TOO APPREHENSIVE TO SHIELD THEM FROM VIOLENCE."[9]

—DAHLIA LITHWICK, LEGAL WRITER AND ANALYST

On occasion, officers fearing for their own lives make fatal mistakes. One such incident was the high-profile 2014 shooting death of a man by police inside an Ohio Walmart. Responding to a call of a man who appeared to have a weapon, police confronted a man carrying what appeared to be a high-powered assault rifle. Only after shooting and killing him did police find the gun was a nearly harmless air rifle made to look like a powerful weapon.

This same type of tragedy could have occurred in Charlottesville, city resident Connor McLean wrote after the August 12 protests. "Perhaps instead of worrying that those rallying would fire the first bullet," he said, "we would have to fear that the police could have." His point was that the lives of thousands of people in Charlottesville that day relied just as heavily on police restraint as on that of armed citizens. During a future demonstration, he theorized, that might not happen: "As police grow more militarized in their armament, they grow increasingly likely to jump into violent situations and to violent action."[10]

McLean also cited a June 2017 study done by several university sociologists that suggests that the more access police have to high-powered, military-style weapons,

Demonstrators protested against police violence toward black people after the 2014 Ohio Walmart shooting.

the more likely they are to use them. McLean's point was that city and state governments must be increasingly careful when faced with circumstances similar to those faced by police in Charlottesville. As the study concluded, disarming demonstrators, rather than continuing to arm police with more and bigger weapons, might be the better option.

DEFENDING FREE SPEECH?

With their loaded assault rifles, camouflage uniforms, combat boots, and helmets, they looked like the US Army or National Guard. They were actually members of the New York Light Foot Militia, an unofficial paramilitary group made up of people from six states. Their mission, they said, was to protect free speech on both sides. Their leader, Christian Yingling, claimed to have spoken to Charlottesville police beforehand and offered to help with security. Yingling said the police welcomed them to attend but couldn't officially invite them.

CHAPTER SEVEN

MEDIA AND PUBLIC REACTION

In the Charlottesville streets, word of the rally's cancellation had spread rapidly through Twitter and text messages. Things began to calm down. Alt-right protesters and counterprotesters began to move away from one another. Police stepped into the gaps and let medical teams move in to tend to the injured. Some people were transported to area hospitals. Given the extent and severity of the fighting, there appeared to have been very few serious injuries.

In the immediate aftermath of the Unite the Right rally, the public and the media reacted with outrage. Some of the outrage was aimed at police and some at

The violence during the rally left many people with minor injuries.

city officials. However, most of it was aimed at the reckless and violent behavior of neo-Nazis and alt-right attendees and organizers at the event. And, as days passed, anger and attention also turned toward President Trump.

During a Saturday afternoon news conference, Trump said, "We condemn in the strongest possible terms this egregious display of hatred, bigotry and violence—on many sides. . . . It's been going on for a long time in our country." He added, "It has no place in America. No citizen should ever fear for their safety and security in our society."[1] It was not so much what the president said, as what he did not say, according to many analysts. Since the 2016 presidential campaign and the election of Trump, he had often been accused of racism, both openly expressed or implied by things he had said or done.

After his comments on Charlottesville, former White

> "THE ESSENCE OF THE ALT-RIGHT CAN BE DISTILLED TO THIS CATCHPHRASE: ALL PEOPLE ARE *NOT* CREATED EQUAL. THAT'S EVEN MORE EXTREME THAN IT MAY SOUND. PROMINENT ALT-RIGHT THINKERS DON'T ONLY BELIEVE THAT SOME ARE NATURALLY TALLER, STRONGER, OR SMARTER THAN OTHERS, BUT ALSO THAT SOME GROUPS ARE MORE DESERVING OF POLITICAL STATUS THAN OTHERS. THEY REJECT THE CONCEPT OF EQUALITY BEFORE THE LAW."[2]
>
> **—THOMAS MAIN, POLITICAL WRITER**

House communications director Anthony Scaramucci said of the president, "I think he needed to be much harsher as it related to the white supremacists and the nature of that. It's actually terrorism and whether it's domestic or international terrorism, with the moral authority of the presidency, you have to call that stuff out." Former vice president Joe Biden commented simply, "There is only one side."[3]

Adding fuel to the fire, neo-Nazi website the Daily Stormer posted remarks praising the president. "Trump's comments were good," the site said. "He didn't attack us. He just said the nation should come together. Nothing specific against us . . . [and he] also refused to answer a question about White Nationalists supporting him. No condemnation at all. When asked to condemn he just walked out of the room. Really, really good. God bless him."[4]

Former KKK grand wizard David Duke also praised

"LOOK AT THE INTENTIONAL COURTING BOTH, ON THE ONE HAND, OF ALL THESE WHITE SUPREMACISTS, WHITE NATIONALIST GROUPS LIKE THAT, ANTI-SEMITIC GROUPS. AND THEN LOOK ON THE OTHER HAND, THE REPEATED FAILURE TO STEP UP, CONDEMN, DENOUNCE, SILENCE . . . PUT TO BED ALL THOSE DIFFERENT EFFORTS."[5]

—CHARLOTTESVILLE MAYOR MICHAEL SIGNER ON TRUMP'S COMMENTS ABOUT THE PROTESTS

Trump for not casting blame on white nationalists. "We are determined to take our country back," he said. "We are going to fulfill the promises of Donald Trump. That's what we believed in, that's why we voted for Donald Trump. Because he said he's going to take our country back."[6]

Trump didn't condemn the white supremacists, nationalists, or neo-Nazis who organized the Charlottesville rally until two days later. Before that, he had also not blamed them for any violence, including the death of activist Heather Heyer. Trump said that people who initiate violence due to racism are criminals, and named the KKK, white supremacists, and neo-Nazis. He also offered condolences to Heyer's family.

Many welcomed the president's words, but others were still not satisfied. Expressing anger that it took

WHITE SUPREMACISTS GET HARASSED

A 1988 episode of the *Oprah Winfrey Show* about neo-Nazi skinheads and the KKK made Daryle Lamont Jenkins angry. He made a list of white supremacists featured on that 1988 talk show broadcast and set about tracking them down. He began gathering information about their leaders and activities. He created a website, One People's Project, to expose and harass them. Through the internet, he persecutes these people by publicly shaming them, posting their pictures, names, addresses, employers, and as much other personal information as he can find. Many people call it harassment, but Jenkins sees it another way. He believes that there should be consequences for hate.

so long for Trump to condemn racists, black political leader and civil rights activist Al Sharpton said Trump's words came too late. Duke disliked the president's words for a different reason. He tweeted to Trump and said the president needed to remember that it was white people who elected him as president.

MORE REACTIONS TO THE PRESIDENT

In the days and weeks following Charlottesville, Trump continued to stir controversy. He repeated his assertions that both protesters and counterprotesters were to blame for the violence. He asked if the counterprotesters felt bad for attacking the alt-right. He also defended the group who had organized the Unite the Right rally as a protest against the removal of the Lee statue. He noted that not everyone involved in the alt-right side of the rally was a neo-Nazi or white supremacist, and that some of the organizers of the rally weren't bad people.

The list of those who disagreed with the president was a long one. They included many leaders of his own Republican Party, including Speaker of the House Paul Ryan. "We cannot allow this old evil to be resurrected,"

Ryan tweeted. "We must be clear. White supremacy is repulsive. This bigotry is counter to all this country stands for. There can be no moral ambiguity."[7]

The number of voices raised in defense and support of the president were few. But someone who did support the president's views was journalist Deroy Murdock. Murdock wrote in an online editorial, "Even though he faces second-degree murder charges, surprisingly little of the national media and [others'] fury is directed at Fields and his actions. Instead, the bitterness is pointed fully at Trump and his words—as poorly chosen and ill-timed as some of them were—as if the president of the United States, and not a 20-year-old bloodthirsty racist, were behind the wheel of that deadly Dodge Challenger."[8]

Others agreed. The facts indicated, they said, that many counterprotesters did indeed

Some people blamed both sides of protesters for the violence that erupted at the rally.

come to Charlottesville determined to fight. Many shouted insults and spat. They threw rocks and foul-smelling liquids at alt-right protesters. Many engaged in fistfights, swung clubs and sticks, and even waved guns. Some were arrested and some—such as civil rights activists Cornel West and Reverend Traci Blackmon, who traveled to Charlottesville specifically for that purpose—were disappointed when they weren't.

Some reporters, such as *Time* magazine's Katy Steinmetz, were convinced that antifa was responsible for at least some of the violence in Charlottesville. She pointed out that it had been a secret for some time that people who call themselves antifa are committed to opposing racist organizations' strong-arm tactics with physical intimidation and violent actions of their own. As other reporters suggested, Trump's much-criticized initial statement that the violence in Charlottesville came from both sides was accurate simply because antifa was there.

In a 2017 *Time* magazine interview, one antifa member defined antifa's cause as being against sexism and racism while protecting the oppressed population. Another said that antifa activists are simply against the idea that the elite can control people. Pamela Oliver, a sociology professor at the University of Wisconsin, has studied

Antifa activists don't have a centralized leadership, but they have developed a logo for their group.

antifa's purposes and tactics. "In the 1930s," she explains, "the Nazis used violence to intimidate people. Antifa argues that if people resisted them then, the fascists wouldn't have gotten so big." But she also points out that antifa's forceful methods might be too extreme for its own good. "Most people think that non-violence is the way to go and that violent, aggressive responses could backfire, that is play into the hands of white supremacists by using violence."[9]

Evidence of such an effect could be seen in the vigorous online discussion among alt-right groups in the days and weeks before Charlottesville. In one post, Kessler urged people to attend and provoke the antifa into violence.

How some people viewed the events in Charlottesville was influenced by their political and social perspectives. Social media provided an outlet for people to express their views and to even offer ways to become actively involved.

FROM THE
HEADLINES

TO KNEEL,
OR NOT TO KNEEL?

In 2016, National Football League (NFL) San Francisco 49ers quarterback Colin Kaepernick drew national attention when he took a knee during the national anthem before a football game to protest a nation that abuses black people. During the 2017 football season, especially after Charlottesville and Trump's controversial remarks, other players followed Kaepernick's example.

The president lashed out through Twitter, urging the NFL to fire any players who are discourteous to the American flag. In response, players and even some coaches and owners began kneeling, linking arms, or lifting fists in protest. Many people didn't like their actions. At some games fans booed players who kneit. Others followed the president's advice and walked out of stadiums or burned their teams' jerseys. A survey conducted in September 2017 by Seton Hall University revealed a somewhat different viewpoint. Results showed that 84 percent of people polled believed in the players' constitutional right to protest. Still, only 35 percent supported the specific protest of kneeling during the anthem and 16 percent thought kneeling players should be cut from their teams.[10]

Colin Kaepernick, *center*, was the first person to kneel during the national anthem, and some of his teammates joined him.

CHAPTER EIGHT

CITIZEN
JOURNALISTS

C ell phone video and eyewitness accounts later led to the arrest of some people charged with committing violent acts during the protests. One alt-right protester was charged with criminal assault for the brutal beating of an African American man and another for shooting a handgun in the direction of counterprotesters.

Citizen journalism played a major role in the Charlottesville turmoil. That term refers to a type of on-the-scene, first-hand coverage of major news events by nonprofessionals. It was often used to describe the raw and uncensored words and images that emerged during 2011's anti-government Arab Spring protests in Tunisia, Syria, and other Middle Eastern nations.

Citizen journalists can catch events that law enforcement officials might miss.

DOXXING

After Charlottesville, some people were victims of doxxing. The term refers to publicly identifying people who wish to remain anonymous on certain websites on which giving one's real name is not required or advisable. People who post other people's addresses, phone numbers, and employer information can expose the victims of doxxing to embarrassment, ridicule, or even physical attack. Many believe doxxing is unethical, even criminal, and some social media platforms, including Reddit and Twitter, consider it a violation of their rules.

"Everyone on the scene is a citizen journalist," an Egyptian professor said during protests in Cairo.[1] The network director of news channel Al Jazeera, Wadah Khanfar, recalled how "we suddenly had 4,000 people on the streets reporting for us, up-loading photos, videos, eyewitness accounts."[2]

In recent years, many people have come to rely on Twitter, Facebook, YouTube, and other online outlets for news. Posted images and comments are often shocking and powerful. But people wonder if the images are always fully accurate presentations of what's really happening.

The problem was clearly illustrated in the aftermath of the Charlottesville protests. One danger of posting amateur, on-the-spot videos on social media is that once they're launched into cyberspace, the images can be manipulated by people. Anyone can edit them, add comments, and warp and bend their meaning.

That happened to Charlottesville resident Brennan Gilmore. He was videotaping his fellow counterprotesters at exactly the moment the car slammed into the crowd. The shocking video he posted went viral. Almost immediately, rumors began swirling online that Gilmore was part of a conspiracy with the car's driver. Neo-Nazi sites said the attack had been staged by the alt-left in order to make the alt-right look like crazed killers. Another site claimed Gilmore and Fields were hired assassins that were part of some dark leftist operation to turn public opinion against the right and overthrow the president. The accusations even got threatening. When someone posted Gilmore's name and address, people began sending him death threats.

AMATEUR DETECTIVES

Similar things can happen even when the most well-intentioned people attempt to interpret online video posts. In the hours after Charlottesville, dozens of self-appointed amateur detectives began studying social media posts, trying to identify the people demonstrating with alt-right protesters. A Twitter account with the name @YesYoureRacist sparked controversy after urging its hundreds of thousands of followers to identify by name white nationalist and supremacist protesters during the protests and violence in Charlottesville.

In a few cases, that sort of crowd scanning produced the desired result. One alt-right rally participant was forced to resign from his restaurant job in Berkeley, California, after online vigilantes identified him in pictures from Charlottesville. Another man, similarly outed, was disowned by his entire family in a letter to a North Dakota newspaper.

There were near-tragic mistakes as well. In one case, investigators mistakenly identified the wrong man as the driver of the car that plowed into crowds in Charlottesville. They tracked the license plate number seen in online pictures to the man who had once

CELL PHONE VIDEO LEADS TO ARRESTS

Cell phone footage taken in Charlottesville showed DeAndre Harris, a 20-year-old African American man, trying to escape as he was attacked. He collapsed and got up several times as a group of white men continued to hammer him with metal flagpoles, umbrellas, and plastic shields. Two weeks after Harris's attack in Charlottesville, on August 12, police arrested 18-year-old Daniel Borden after someone identified him from the cell phone video. Friends said Borden had been obsessed with Nazis and racial violence since middle school and belonged to a gang called Brothers of the Confederacy. Four others, including Jacob Scott Goodwin, were also identified. Goodwin was convicted by a jury in Charlottesville of "malicious wounding" in May 2018.[3]

owned the car and sold it. After they posted his name and address online, the man received multiple threats. Police even advised him and his family to leave home until the confusion could be cleared up.

Then there was the case of the bearded man seen in Charlottesville protest photos wearing a shirt with the words "Arkansas Engineering."[4] Amateur detectives Googled the phrase and looked for someone who matched the face of the person they saw marching with neo-Nazis. On the website of the Engineering Research Center at the University of Arkansas, they spotted bearded Kyle Quinn and labeled him online as a white supremacist. Quinn, a research worker with no links to such politics, was flooded with obscene messages and threats on Twitter and Instagram. Countless people called and texted, demanding he quit his job. They posted his home address on social networks. His colleagues and employer knew he was not the person in the photos. But Quinn still was faced with explaining that to multitudes of angry strangers. Many people were thoroughly convinced that he was a white supremacist because they'd seen it stated as a fact online.

Recording a brief moment of an event doesn't always capture the whole story.

Professional journalists do sometimes make the same mistakes. But the majority of reputable media outlets, print and digital, go to extreme lengths to correctly identify anyone in the photos they publish. They have the money, staff, and time to confirm facts and faces before they publish information. Many online sites don't, and neither do amateur investigators.

IMPACT OF CHARLOTTESVILLE

On October 12, 2017, Charlottesville city leaders filed a lawsuit against individuals including Kessler and Spencer. The lawsuit also charged members of a number of militia groups. Among those listed were the leftist Redneck Revolt and extreme right groups such as Vanguard

America and League of the South. Mayor Signer said the suit was an attempt to stop future battles between white nationalists and extreme leftists in his city.

Another effect of Charlottesville was a resurgence of activity by Black Lives Matter. Members were certainly present in Charlottesville on August 12, 2017, but they found themselves woefully outnumbered and unprepared for the level of violence they encountered there.

The Charlottesville protests also brought into sharp focus some of the most divisive and troubling issues facing US society. First is the sometimes violent conflict between extreme left and right political factions. Second is the continuing conversation concerning racial equality. Part of that issue—and a key factor in sparking the Charlottesville disturbance—is the argument over what to do with Confederate monuments and symbols in public spaces. In addition, the protests illustrated that vitally important issues concerning gun control, private militias, and citizens' First and Second Amendment rights are still unresolved and divisive.

ESSENTIAL
FACTS

MAJOR EVENTS

- A vote by the Charlottesville City Council to remove the Robert E. Lee statue from Emancipation Park sparked a strong reaction from the alt-right.

- Members of the alt-right decided to demonstrate their opposition to the removal of the Robert E. Lee statue. They organized the Unite the Right rally for August 12, 2017.

- The night before the rally, there were clashes by protesters and counterprotesters on the University of Virginia campus.

- On the day of the Unite the Right rally, protesters and counterprotesters fought once again. A woman named Heather Heyer was killed.

- President Donald Trump faced backlash after refusing to place exclusive blame on any group in the protests at first.

KEY PLAYERS

- The Charlottesville City Council's efforts to remove the Robert E. Lee statue from Emancipation Park drew extreme right protesters and anti-fascist counterprotesters into direct conflict. Mayor Mike Signer and members of the Charlottesville City Council were faced with the task of leading their community during the protests.

- Jason Kessler, a Charlottesville resident and white supremacist, was perhaps the most vocal and active opponent to the city's effort to remove the Confederate statue.

IMPACT ON SOCIETY

The Charlottesville protests brought left and extreme right political ideologies to the national spotlight. They showed that some people in the United States believe white nationalism is something the country should strive for, while others oppose this idea. The protests also highlighted the argument over Confederate symbols and monuments and what governments should do about them.

QUOTE

"These monuments celebrate a fictional, sanitized Confederacy ignoring the death, ignoring the enslavement, ignoring the terror that it actually stood for."

—Mitch Landrieu, mayor of New Orleans, 2017

GLOSSARY

ALT-RIGHT

Short for *alternative right*; the name is sometimes used to describe people who aggressively support white supremacist and white nationalist causes.

AMBIGUITY

Doubtfulness or lack of clarity, usually referring to language.

CONFEDERATE

Having to do with the culture or beliefs of the former Confederate States of America.

DESEGREGATION

The elimination of laws, customs, or practices under which people from different religions, ancestries, or ethnic groups are restricted to specific or separate public facilities, neighborhoods, schools, or organizations.

EGREGIOUS

Extraordinarily shocking and bad.

FASCIST

A person who believes in a government structure in which one person has total power and opposition is suppressed.

MILITIA

A military force made up of nonprofessional fighters.

WHITE NATIONALIST

A person who supports the establishment of a separate nation or state for the people of the white, Caucasian race, and the exclusion of everyone else.

WHITE SUPREMACIST

Someone who believes that white people are superior to all other races.

ADDITIONAL
RESOURCES

SELECTED BIBLIOGRAPHY

"Empty Pedestals: What Should Be Done with Civic Monuments to the Confederacy and Its Leaders?" *HistoryNet*, Oct. 2017, history.net. Accessed 20 Apr. 2018.

Heim, Joe. "Recounting a Day of Rage, Hate, Violence and Death." *Washington Post*, 14 Aug. 2017, washingtonpost.com. Accessed 20 Apr. 2018.

Spencer, Hawes. "A Far-Right Gathering Bursts into Brawls." *New York Times*, 13 Aug. 2017, nytimes.com. Accessed 20 Apr. 2018.

FURTHER READINGS

Bakshi, Kelly. *Roots of Racism*. Abdo, 2018.

Hamen, Susan E. *Civil War Aftermath and Reconstruction*. Abdo, 2017.

ONLINE RESOURCES

Booklinks
NONFICTION NETWORK
FREE! ONLINE NONFICTION RESOURCES

To learn more about the Charlottesville protests, visit
abdobooklinks.com. These links are routinely monitored and
updated to provide the most current information available.

MORE INFORMATION

For more information on this subject, contact or visit the
following organizations:

National Civil Rights Museum
450 Mulberry Street
Memphis, TN 38103
901-521-9699
civilrightsmuseum.org
The National Civil Rights Museum teaches visitors about the civil rights
movement.

Southern Poverty Law Center
400 Washington Avenue
Montgomery, AL 36104
888-414-7752
splcenter.org
The Southern Poverty Law Center is a nonprofit organization that fights
bigotry. The group also fights for justice for underserved people in the
United States.

SOURCE NOTES

CHAPTER 1. UNITE THE RIGHT

1. Joe Heim. "Recounting a Day of Rage, Hate, Violence and Death." *Washington Post*, 14 Aug. 2017, washingtonpost.com. Accessed 12 July 2018.

2. Jason Wilson. "Charlottesville: Far-Right Crowd with Torches Encircles Counter-Protest Group." *Guardian*, 12 Aug. 2017, theguardian.com. Accessed 12 July 2018.

3. Adam Epstein. "'Blood and Soil': The Meaning of the Nazi Slogan Chanted by White Nationalists in Charlottesville." *Quartz*, 13 Aug. 2017, qz.com. Accessed 12 July 2018.

4. Jessica Chia. "Brawls Erupt as Torch-Wielding White Supremacists March through University of Virginia Campus." *New York Daily News*, 12 Aug. 2017, nydailynews.com. Accessed 12 July 2018.

5. Mike Signer. "Statement on the Rally at the University of Virginia." *Facebook*, 11 Aug. 2017, facebook.com. Accessed 12 July 2018.

6. Alexis Gravely, et al. "Torch-Wielding White Nationalists March at U.Va." *Cavalier Daily*, 12 Aug. 2017, cavalierdaily.com. Accessed 12 July 2018.

CHAPTER 2. STEPS TO THE CONFLICT

1. Hawes Spencer and Sheryl Gay Stolberg. "White Nationalists March on University of Virginia." *New York Times*, 11 Aug. 2017, nytimes.com. Accessed 12 July 2018.

2. Hawes Spencer. "A Far-Right Gathering Bursts into Brawls." *New York Times*, 13 Aug. 2017, nytimes.com. Accessed 12 July 2018.

3. Sarah Viets. "Neo-Nazi Misfits Join Unite the Right." *Southern Poverty Law Center*, 26 July 2017, splcenter.org. Accessed 12 July 2018.

4. Ed Ayers. "Monumental Disagreements." *Backstory*, 24 May 2013, backstoryradio.org. Accessed 12 July 2018.

5. Jacey Fortin. "The Statue at the Center of Charlottesville's Storm." *New York Times*, 13 Aug. 2017, nytimes.com. Accessed 12 July 2018.

6. Jaclyn Piermarini. "City Council to Consider Lee-Jackson Day." *CBS News*, 28 Jan. 2015, cbs19news.com. Accessed 12 July 2018.

7. Dean Stevens. "Charlottesville, VA to Consider Dropping Lee-Jackson City Holiday." *Sons of Confederate Veterans*, 31 Jan. 2015, scscv.com. Accessed 12 July 2018.

8. Jason Horowitz, Nick Corasaniti, and Ashley Southall. "Nine Killed in Shooting at Black Church in Charleston." *New York Times*, 17 June 2015, nytimes.com. Accessed 12 July 2018.

9. Meredith Hamilton. "Confederate Battle Flag: Why South Carolina Lawmakers May Vote to Keep It." *Christian Science Monitor*, 6 July 2015, csmonitor.com. Accessed 12 July 2018.

10. "CNN/ORC International Poll." *Turner*, 2 July 2015, turner.com. Accessed 12 July 2018.

11. Stephanie McCrummen and Elehe Izadi. "Confederate Flag Comes Down on South Carolina's Statehouse Grounds." *Washington Post*, 19 July 2015, washingtonpost.com. Accessed 12 July 2018.

12. Harriet Alexander. "'Our Great Country Being Ripped Apart': Donald Trump Criticises 'Foolish' Removal of Confederate Monuments in New Tweets." *Telegraph*, 17 Aug. 2017, telegraph.co.uk. Accessed 12 July 2018.

13. Esther Ciammachilli. "In Birmingham, the Debate over Confederate Monuments Is Renewed after Charlottesville." *NPR*, 17 Aug. 2017, npr.org. Accessed 12 July 2018.

14. Lauren Berg. "Charlottesville Police Investigating Vandalism of Robert E. Lee Statue." *Daily Progress*, 30 June 2015, dailyprogress.com. Accessed 12 July 2018.

15. Janelle Ross. "'They Were Not Patriots': New Orleans Removes Monument to Confederate Gen. Robert E. Lee." *Washington Post*, 19 May 2017, washingtonpost.com. Accessed 12 July 2018.

16. Zyahna Bryant. "Change the Name of Lee Park and Remove the Statue." *Change*, n.d., change.org. Accessed 12 July 2018.

17. Karen L. Cox. "White Supremacy Is the Whole Point of Confederate Statues." *Washington Post*, 18 Aug. 2017, washingtonpost.com. Accessed 12 July 2018.

18. "A Report on Public Symbols of the Confederacy." *Southern Poverty Law Center*, 21 Apr. 2016, splcenter.org. Accessed 12 July 2018.

19. Andrea Lannom. "Monumental Debate." *Register-Herald*, 10 Sept. 2017, register-herald.com. Accessed 12 July 2018.

20. Cox, "White Supremacy Is the Whole Point of Confederate Statues."

21. "A Report on Public Symbols of the Confederacy."

22. "Empty Pedestals: What Should Be Done with Civic Monuments to the Confederacy and Its Leaders?" *Civil War Times*, Oct. 2017, history.net. Accessed 12 July 2018.

23. "Blue Ribbon Commission on Race, Memorials and Public Spaces: Report to City Council." *City of Charlottesville*, 19 Dec. 2016, charlottesville.org. Accessed 12 July 2018.

24. Jonathan McFadden and Langston Taylor. "Charlotte's Confederate Monument Stirred Passions, Then and Now." *Charlottesville Observer*, 17 July 2017, charlotteobserver.com. Accessed 12 July 2018.

25. Madison Park. "Why White Nationalists Are Drawn to Charlottesville." *CNN*, 12 Aug. 2017, cnn.com. Accessed 12 July 2018.

26. Brandon Griggs. "Protests over Confederate Statue Shake Charlottesville, Virginia." *CNN*, 15 May 2017, cnn.com. Accessed 12 July 2018.

27. Maya Rhodan. "Virginia Mayor: Protest Supporting Confederate Statues 'Harkens Back to Days of KKK.'" *Time*, 15 May 2017, time.com. Accessed 13 July 2018.

28. "Richard Bertrand Spencer." *Southern Poverty Law Center*, n.d., splcenter.org. Accessed 13 July 2018.

29. Lisa Provence. "Show of Force: Police Tear Gas Protesters after KKK Leaves Rally." *C-Ville*, 9 July 2017, c-ville.com. Accessed 13 July 2018.

30. Lilly Workneh. "Bree Newsome, Activist Who Took Down Confederate Flag, Says She Refuses 'To Be Ruled by Fear.'" *Huffington Post*, 30 June 2015, huffingtonpost.com. Accessed 13 July 2018.

CHAPTER 3. LOOKING BACK

1. Ryan Cooper. "How America Forgot the True History of the Civil War." *Week*, 18 Aug. 2017, theweek.com. Accessed 13 July 2018.

2. John Bacon. "UVA President: Student Protesters 'Desecrated' Jefferson Statue." *USA Today*, 14 Sept. 2017, usatoday.com. Accessed 13 July 2018.

3. Bacon, "UVA President: Student Protesters 'Desecrated' Jefferson Statue."

4. Monica Davy. "It Did Happen Here: The Lynching That a City Forgot." *New York Times*, 4 Dec. 2017, nytimes.com. Accessed 13 July 2018.

5. "Clayton Jackson McGhie Memorial Discussion Guide." *Otto Bremer Foundation*, n.d., claytonjacksonmcghie.org. Accessed 13 July 2018.

6. John M. Glionna. "Civil Rights Lawyer Seeks to Commemorate Another Side of Southern Heritage: Lynchings." *Los Angeles Times*, 5 July 2015, latimes.com. Accessed 13 July 2018.

SOURCE NOTES
CONTINUED

7. Derek W. Black. "Charlottesville: A Step in Our Long Arc toward Justice." *Conversation*, 27 Aug. 2017, theconversation.com. Accessed 13 July 2018.

8. "First Amendment." *Cornell Law School*, n.d., law.cornell.edu. Accessed 13 July 2018.

CHAPTER 4. THE PROTEST

1. A. C. Thompson and Karim Hajj. "Clean Cut Frat-Boys Are the New Face of White Supremacists." *Newsweek*, 15 Aug. 2017, newsweek.com. Accessed 13 July 2018.

2. Becca Andrews. "Right to Carry Laws Are Making Violent Protests Like Charlottesville Even Harder to Defuse." *Mother Jones*, 16 Aug. 2017, motherjones.com. Accessed 13 July 2018.

3. David L. Hudson, Jr. "Fighting Words." *Freedom Forum Institute*, July 2009, freedomforuminstitute.org. Accessed 13 July 2018.

4. Ray Sanchez. "Thousands March in Boston in Protest of Controversial Rally." *CNN*, 19 Aug. 2017, cnn.com. Accessed 13 July 2018.

5. Cory Collins. "What Is the 'Alt-Right'?" *Teaching Tolerance*, n.d., tolerance.org. Accessed 13 July 2018.

6. Joe Heim. "Recounting a Day of Rage, Hate, Violence and Death." *Washington Post*, 14 Aug. 2017, washingtonpost.com. Accessed 13 July 2018.

7. Christina Caron. "Heather Heyer, Charlottesville Victim, Is Recalled as 'a Strong Woman.'" *New York Times*, 12 Aug. 2017, nytimes.com. Accessed 13 July 2018.

8. Joe Ruiz. "Ohio Man Charged with Murder in Fatal Car Attack on Anti-White Nationalist March." *NPR*, 13 Aug. 2017, npr.org. Accessed 13 July 2018.

9. Christopher Mathias and Andy Campbell. "How What Happened Here in Charlottesville Was Inevitable." *Huffington Post*, 13 Aug. 2017, huffingtonpost.com. Accessed 13 July 2018.

CHAPTER 5. POLICE AND THE PROTEST

1. "Memorandum Opinion." *In the United States District Court for the Western District of Virginia Charlottesville Division*, n.d., vawd.uscourts.gov. Accessed 13 July 2018.

2. Sheryl Gay Stolberg. "Hurt and Angry, Charlottesville Tries to Regroup from Violence." *New York Times*, 13 Aug. 2017, nytimes.com. Accessed 13 July 2018.

3. Amy B. Wang. "Watch: Charlottesville Counterprotesters Shut Down a White Nationalist's News Conference." *Washington Post*, 13 Aug. 2017, washingtonpost.com. Accessed 13 July 2018.

4. Harriet Sinclair. "Charlottesville Rally Organizer Blames Police for Violence, Claims White Supremacists Were Victimized." *Newsweek*, 13 Aug. 2017, newsweek.com. Accessed 13 July 2018.

5. Robert Zullo. "Virginia Officials Defend Handling of Violent Charlottesville Rally and Counterprotest." *Richmond Times-Dispatch*, 14 Aug. 2017, richmond.com. Accessed 13 July 2018.

6. Zullo, "Virginia Officials Defend Handling of Violent Charlottesville Rally and Counterprotest."

CHAPTER 6. GUNS IN THE STREETS

1. Hawes Spencer. "A Far-Right Gathering Bursts into Brawls." *New York Times*, 13 Aug. 2017, nytimes.com. Accessed 13 July 2018.

2. "Second Amendment." *Cornell Law School*, n.d., law.cornell.edu. Accessed 13 July 2018.

3. Nicole Hensley. "White Supremacists Brandishing Torches Return to Confederate Statue in Charlottesville." *New York Daily News*, 8 Oct. 2017, nydailynews.com. Accessed 13 July 2018.

4. David L. Ulin. "'The Second Amendment' Is a Smart History of Guns and the U.S." *Los Angeles Times*, 23 May 2014, latimes.com. Accessed 13 July 2018.

5. John Paul Stevens. *Six Amendments: How and Why We Should Change the Constitution.* Little, Brown and Company, 2014. 132.

6. "Americans Increasingly Torn over Gun Issues, Survey Shows." *CBS News*, 22 June 2017, cbsnews.com. Accessed 13 July 2018.

7. "The Gunmen at 'Free Speech' Rallies." *New York Times*, 18 Aug. 2017, nytimes.com. Accessed 13 July 2018.

8. John Feinblatt. "Ban the Open Carry of Firearms." *New York Times*, 17 Aug. 2017, nytimes.com. Accessed 13 July 2018.

9. Dahlia Lithwick and Mark Joseph Stern. "The Guns Won." *Slate*, 14 Aug. 2017, slate.com. Accessed 13 July 2018.

10. Connor McLean. "You Don't Need a Gun to Peacefully Protest." *Slate*, 24 Aug. 2017, slate.com. Accessed 13 July 2018.

CHAPTER 7. MEDIA AND PUBLIC REACTION

1. Maria Mercedes Lara. "'There Is Only One Side': Celebrities and Politicians Slam Trump for Response to Charlottesville Violence." *People*, 13 Aug. 2017, people.com. Accessed 13 July 2018.

2. Thomas J. Main. "What's the Alt-Right, and How Large Is Its Audience?" *Los Angeles Times*, 22 Aug. 2017, latimes.com. Accessed 13 July 2018.

3. Lara, "'There Is Only One Side.'"

4. Dominique Mosbergen. "Neo-Nazi Site Daily Stormer Praises Trump's Charlottesville Reaction: 'He Loves Us All.'" *Huffington Post*, 13 Aug. 2017, huffingtonpost.com. Accessed 13 July 2018.

5. Eli Watkins. "Charlottesville Mayor on Trump: 'Look at the Campaign He Ran.'" *CNN*, 13 Aug. 2017, cnn.com. Accessed 13 July 2018.

6. Mosbergen, "Neo-Nazi Site Daily Stormer Praises Trump's Charlottesville Reaction."

7. Andrew O'Reilly. "Antifa Violence Leaves Leftists to Question Whether Movement Hurts or Helps." *Fox News*, 30 Aug. 2017, foxnews.com. Accessed 13 July 2018.

8. Deroy Murdock. "Both Sides Were to Blame for Charlottesville Violence." *Union Leader*, 17 Aug. 2017, nhangle.com. Accessed 13 July 2018.

9. O'Reilly, "Antifa Violence Leaves Leftists to Question Whether Movement Hurts or Helps."

10. Daniel Roberts. "Poll: 84% Support NFL Players' Right to Protest." *Yahoo Finance*, 28 Sept. 2017, finance.yahoo.com. Accessed 13 July 2018.

CHAPTER 8. CITIZEN JOURNALISTS

1. David Batty. "Arab Spring Leads Surge in Events Captured on Cameraphones." *Guardian*, 29 Dec. 2011, theguardian.com. Accessed 13 July 2018.

2. Colleen Gillard and Georgia Wells. "How the Arab Spring Has Transformed Journalism." *ARIJ*, n.d., en.arij.net. Accessed 13 July 2018.

3. Emily Shugerman. "White Supremacist Found Guilty of Assaulting Black Man at Charlottesville 'Unite the Right' Rally." *Independent*, 2 May 2018, independent.co.uk. Accessed 13 July 2018.

4. Daniel Victor. "Amateur Sleuths Aim to Identify Charlottesville Marchers, But Sometimes Misfire." *New York Times*, 14 Aug. 2017, nytimes.com. Accessed 13 July 2018.

INDEX

ABOUT THE
AUTHORS

MICHAEL CAPEK

Michael Capek lives in northern Kentucky near Cincinnati, Ohio. He's a former teacher and the author of many articles, stories, and nonfiction books for young readers.

DUCHESS HARRIS, JD, PHD

Professor Harris is the chair of the American Studies department at Macalester College and curator of the Duchess Harris Collection of ABDO books. She is the author and coauthor of recently released ABDO books including *Hidden Human Computers: The Black Women of NASA*, *Black Lives Matter*, and *Race and Policing*.

Before working with ABDO, she authored several other books on the topics of race, culture, and American history. She served as an associate editor for *Litigation News*, the American Bar Association Section of Litigation's quarterly flagship publication, and was the first editor in chief of *Law Raza*, an interactive online journal covering race and the law, published at William Mitchell College of Law. She has earned a PhD in American Studies from the University of Minnesota and a JD from William Mitchell College of Law.